I0020621

FORWARD/COMMENTARY

The National Institute of Standards and Technology (NIST) is a measurement standards laboratory, and a non-regulatory agency of the United States Department of Commerce. Its mission is to promote innovation and industrial competitiveness. Founded in 1901, as the National Bureau of Standards, NIST was formed with the mandate to provide standard weights and measures, and to serve as the national physical laboratory for the United States. With a world-class measurement and testing laboratory encompassing a wide range of areas of computer science, mathematics, statistics, and systems engineering, NIST's cybersecurity program supports its overall mission to promote U.S. innovation and industrial competitiveness by advancing measurement science, standards, and related technology through research and development in ways that enhance economic security and improve our quality of life.

The need for cybersecurity standards and best practices that address interoperability, usability and privacy has been shown to be critical for the nation. NIST's cybersecurity programs seek to enable greater development and application of practical, innovative security technologies and methodologies that enhance the country's ability to address current and future computer and information security challenges.

The cybersecurity publications produced by NIST cover a wide range of cybersecurity concepts that are carefully designed to work together to produce a holistic approach to cybersecurity primarily for government agencies and constitute the best practices used by industry. This holistic strategy to cybersecurity covers the gamut of security subjects from development of secure encryption standards for communication and storage of information while at rest to how best to recover from a cyber-attack.

Why buy a book you can download for free?

Some are available only in electronic media. Some online docs are missing pages or barely legible.

We at 4th Watch Books are former government employees, so we know how government employees actually use the standards. When a new standard is released, an engineer prints it out, punches holes and puts it in a 3-ring binder. While this is not a big deal for a 5 or 10-page document, many NIST documents are over 100 pages and printing a large document is a time-consuming effort. So, an engineer that's paid $75 an hour is spending hours simply printing out the tools needed to do the job. That's time that could be better spent doing engineering. We publish these documents so engineers can focus on what they were hired to do – engineering. It's much more cost-effective to just order the latest version from Amazon.com

If there is a standard you would like published, let us know. Our web site is Cybah.webplus.net

Please see the Cybersecurity Standards list at the end of this book.

CyberSecurity Standards Library™

Get a Complete Library of Over 300 Cybersecurity Standards on 1 Convenient DVD!

The **4th Watch CyberSecurity Standards Library** is a DVD disc that puts over 300 current and archived cybersecurity standards from NIST, DOD, DHS, CNSS and NERC at your fingertips! Many of these cybersecurity standards are hard to find and we included the current version and a previous version for many of them. The DVD includes four books written by Luis Ayala: **The Cyber Dictionary, Cybersecurity Standards, Cyber-Security Glossary of Building Hacks and Cyber-Attacks**, and **Cyber-Physical Attack Defenses: Preventing Damage to Buildings and Utilities**.

- ✓ DVD includes many Hard-to-find Cybersecurity Standards - some still in Draft.
- ✓ Docs are organized by source and listed numerically so each standard is easy to locate.
- ✓ The listing of standards on the DVD includes an abstract of the subject, and date issued.
- ✓ PDF format for use on PC, Mac, eReaders, or tablets.
- ✓ No need for WiFi / Internet.
- ✓ Save countless hours of searching and downloading.
- ✓ Carry in a briefcase - terrific for travel.

4th Watch Publishing is releasing the CyberSecurity Standards Library DVD to make it easier for you to access the tools you need to ensure the security of your computer networks and SCADA systems. We also publish many of these standards on demand so you don't need to waste valuable time searching for the latest version of a standard, printing hundreds of pages and punching holes so they can go in a three-ring binder. **Order on Amazon.com**

The DVD works on PC and Mac with the standards in PDF format. To view the CyberSecurity Standards Library on the DVD, a computer with a DVD drive is required. The most current version of your internet browser, at least 2GB of RAM, and current version of Adobe Reader is recommended. (Compatible browsers include Internet Explorer 8+, Mozilla Firefox 4+, Apple Safari 5+, Google Chrome 15+)

NISTIR 8135

Identifying and Categorizing Data Types for Public Safety Mobile Applications:

Workshop Report

Michael Ogata

This publication is available free of charge from:
http://dx.doi.org/10.6028/NIST.IR.8135

National Institute of
Standards and Technology
U.S. Department of Commerce

NISTIR 8135

Identifying and Categorizing Data Types for Public Safety Mobile Applications:

Workshop Report

Michael Ogata
Software and Systems Division
Information Technology Laboratory

This publication is available free of charge from:
http://dx.doi.org/10.6028/NIST.IR.8135

May 2016

U.S. Department of Commerce
Penny Pritzker, Secretary

National Institute of Standards and Technology
Willie May, Under Secretary of Commerce for Standards and Technology and Director

National Institute of Standards and Technology Interagency or Internal Report 8135
40 pages (May 2016)

This publication is available free of charge from:
http://dx.doi.org/10.6028/NIST.IR.8135

Comments on this publication may be submitted to:

National Institute of Standards and Technology
Attn: Applied Cybersecurity Division, Information Technology Laboratory
100 Bureau Drive (Mail Stop 2000) Gaithersburg, MD 20899-2000
Email: mobile_app_data_types@nist.gov

All comments are subject to release under the Freedom of Information Act (FOIA).

Reports on Computer Systems Technology

The Information Technology Laboratory (ITL) at the National Institute of Standards and Technology (NIST) promotes the U.S. economy and public welfare by providing technical leadership for the Nation's measurement and standards infrastructure. ITL develops tests, test methods, reference data, proof of concept implementations, and technical analyses to advance the development and productive use of information technology. ITL's responsibilities include the development of management, administrative, technical, and physical standards and guidelines for the cost-effective security and privacy of other than national security-related information in federal information systems.

Abstract

The Association of Public-Safety Communications (APCO), in cooperation with FirstNet and the Department of Commerce held a half-day workshop on June 2, 2015, "Identifying and Categorizing Data Types for Public Safety Mobile Applications." The goal of this workshop was to begin identifying different types of data that will flow through applications that operate on the National Public Safety Broadband Network (NPSBN). A diverse group of first responders, industry leaders, and government representatives attended the workshop. This document describes the workshop and captures the input received from the workshop attendees.

Keywords

communication; cybersecurity; first responders; FirstNet; mobile applications; public safety

Acknowledgements

This publication was developed as part of the NTIA/NIST Public Safety Communication Research (PSCR) program with sponsorship from the Office for Interoperability and Compatibility (OIC) at the Department of Homeland Security (DHS). The author of this document would like to thank Jeff Cohen and Mark Reddish from the Association of Public-Safety Communication Officials (APCO), Mark Golaszewski of First Responder Network Authority (FirstNet) and Ray Lehr for their help organizing and proctoring the workshop.

The organizers and attendees would also like to extend their gratitude to United States Coast Guard Sector San Diego for the use of their facilities during the course of the workshop.

Audience

This document is intended for members of the public safety community. It is also intended for mobile application developers who are interested in building applications for the public safety domain.

Trademark Information

Table of Contents

List of Appendices

List of Figures

List of Tables

1   Introduction

1.1   Overview

The Association of Public-Safety Communications (APCO), in cooperation with FirstNet and the Department of Commerce held a half-day workshop on June 2, 2015, "Identifying and Categorizing Data Types for Public Safety Mobile Applications." The workshop was held at the Untied States Cost Guard Sector San Diego facility in San Diego, California. Its primary goal was to identify different types of data that will be used by the mobile applications that will operate on the National Public Safety Broadband Network (NPSBN). The workshop's second objective was to examine how these data types influence the cybersecurity posture of a public safety organization. Approximately 50 participants provided input to the workshop. These attendees came from a diverse background of expertise, hailing from fire and emergency medical services (EMS), law enforcement, the telecom industry, federal and local governments, and academia.

1.2   Workshop Organizers

The "Identifying and Categorizing Data Types for Public Safety Mobile Applications" workshop was organized and planned by representatives from APCO and the Department of Commerce. Each of the workshop organizers has a vested interest in ensuring that public safety mobile applications are developed to meet the functional, security, and usability needs of the public safety community.

APCO is the world's oldest and largest organization of public safety communications professionals. Its members include state and local employees of law enforcement, fire, and emergency medical service departments. APCO serves public safety communications practitioners by providing professional development, technical assistance, advocacy, training, and outreach. In addition, APCO is an American National Standards Institute (ANSI) accredited standards developer.

The Department of Commerce is home to the Public Safety Communications Research (PSCR) program, a joint program run by the National Telecommunications and Information Administration (NTIA) and the National Institute of Standards and Technology (NIST). PSCR performs research, development, testing, and evaluation to foster nationwide public safety communications interoperability on behalf of their sponsors at the Department of Homeland Security (DHS) Office of Interoperability and Compatibility (OIC)/Office of Emergency Communication (OEC) and First Responder Network Authority (FirstNet). Working with public safety organizations (e.g., APCO and the National Public Safety Telecommunications Council (NPSTC)), PSCR draws on public safety communications requirements provided by public safety practitioners to ground efforts in the needs of the public safety community. In 2013, PSCR began cybersecurity research efforts related to public safety communications including public safety mobile application security.

1.3   Document Structure

The remainder of this document captures the background and output of the workshop. Section 2 describes the goals and reasoning behind why this workshop was held. It also provides the historical context of how the workshop satisfies the recommendations of previous work concerning mobile application security. Section 3 explains the methodology used by the workshop organizers to develop the workshop activities. Section 4 describes the workshop activities and structure. Section 5 relates the data types that were identified and categorized as part of the workshop proceedings. Appendix A— details the workshop scenarios supplied to the attendees. These scenarios were used to frame the discussions held during the workshop.

2. Workshop Background

2.1 Overview

Mobile applications that run on Long Term Evolution (LTE) devices will feature an increasingly prominent role in public safety. The data processed by these applications will factor into a public safety organization's cybersecurity posture. This section describes the motivations behind why the organizers felt this workshop was beneficial to the public safety community including supporting work and documentation that support these motivations.

The Middle Class Tax Relief Act of 2012 mandated the creation of the nation's first nationwide public safety broadband network (NPSBN). This legislation also created the First Responder Network Authority (FirstNet) whose role it is to build and maintain the NPSBN. The goal of the NPSBN is to provide public safety and first responders with modern and interoperable access to information and services. The NPSBN will be built using LTE technology. This new network will be accessed by a diverse ecosystem of devices. A mixture of commercial off-the-shelf (COTS) and special purpose LTE devices will utilize the NPSBN. The mobile applications that will run on those devices will be an important vehicle to deliver data and services to public safety personnel. These applications will also have specific cybersecurity requirements that will set them apart from mobile applications targeted at the general consumer market.

The workshop described in this document was designed to utilize the domain knowledge of public safety officials to list the types of data that will be handled by the mobile applications that serve their needs. More specifically it supports the creation of a publicly maintained data dictionary of data types for public safety mobile applications. A data dictionary is a canonically maintained list of data type names and their associated definitions. It is also meant to be a medium to relate how each of these data types impact cybersecurity from the perspective of public safety organizations. The creation of a data dictionary for public safety fulfills two needs. First, it fulfills a recommendation made by PSCR, NIST, and APCO during the output of the previous workshop. Second, it supports and enables several recommendations made by FirstNet. The remainder of this section provides a brief overview of these two areas.

2.2 Previous Workshop

To better define and explore how cybersecurity relates to public safety PSCR, APCO, and NIST have engaged directly with the public safety community through a series of workshops. The first such workshop, "Public Safety Mobile Application Security Requirements," was held in February 2014. That workshop and its findings are summarized in NIST Interagency Report (NISTIR) 8018 [5]. Its goal was to explore how public safety specific security requirements on mobile applications will be unique for public safety when compared to other mobile application markets. Due to the often life-critical nature of public safety, it will be clear that mobile applications for public safety will have stringent requirements for information security, reliability, and usability. This workshop focused on six areas:

- Battery Life,
- Unintentional Denial of Service (DoS),

- Mobile Application Vetting,
- Location Information,
- Data Protection, and
- Identity Management.

NISTIR 8018 establishes recommendations as well as describes further areas of research for each of these topics. Public safety has unique requirements on data when compared to the consumer mobile application market space. Public safety applications may handle sensitive information concerning active investigations. They may process private medical data or maintain a record of a public safety official's geographic location. NISTIR 8018 captured the desire of public safety officials to have a structured and consistent approach to data protection. It proposes multiple solutions for this approach. At a minimum, it states the application developers must make declarations as to what data their applications handle and what mechanisms or techniques they use to safeguard that data. However, it also recognized that without a codified way to describe public safety data, even this minimal requirement may fail to meet public safety's needs. NISTIR 8018 therefore recommends the creation of a public safety data dictionary to enumerate and define public safety data types.

2.3 Recommendations by FirstNet

This data dictionary would also serve to support recommendations made by FirstNet. FirstNet understands the importance of incorporating cybersecurity into the foundations of the NPSBN. The request for proposal (RFP) that defines how the network will be constructed pays special consideration to defining best practices and recommendations concerning mobile application security. Specific recommendations concerning public safety mobile applications can be found in Appendix C-10, "NPSBN Cyber Security," of the NPSBN RFP [2]. These recommendations include, but are not limited to the following:

- Evaluation and certification of application developers;
- Analysis and certification of applications;
- Ensuring applications protect data while at rest, in use, and in transit; and
- Ensuring proper logging of applications and user actions.

A data dictionary enables these recommendations. Well-defined data types improve the accuracy of application analysis and certification. They better define policy concerning what data should and should not be retained in application logs and for how long that data is preserved. It provides a mechanism for evaluating application developers' understanding of the public safety domain. Finally, it defines what requirements applications must fulfill concerning what and how data is protected.

2.4 Additional Motivations

In addition to these two areas, proactive identification of public safety-specific data and information types strengthens public safety's security posture in several ways. First, it provides a common language for deriving the functional and security requirements of public safety applications. This strengthens public safety organizations by helping them clearly state their requirements to application developers. It also improves an organization's ability to compare and contrast mobile applications both within their organization but also between other organizations. Second, it familiarizes the mobile application development community with public safety's mission and domain requirements. Finally, knowing the data, and the value of the data, helps organizations to select and develop security controls and capabilities needed to protect that data.

3. Workshop Methodology

3.1 Overview

The main goal of the workshop was to identify data types that will be handled by public safety mobile devices and discuss how those data types will influence the security requirements enforced on public safety mobile applications. This section describes the methodology that served as inspiration for the workshop's activities. First, NIST Federal Information Processing Standard (FIPS) 199, *Standards for Security Categorization of Federal Information and Information Systems* [7], is discussed. FIPS 199 provides clarification for how the workshop organizers defined an information type. It then describes the process of determining an information type's relationship with cybersecurity risk and how those relationships can be used to describe the cybersecurity risk of information systems. Then, the NIST Risk Management Framework is used to examine how security categorization fits into a larger cybersecurity posture. Next, NIST Special Publication (SP) 800-60 Volume I Revision 1, *Guide for Mapping Types of Information and Information Systems to Security Categories* [6], further defines information types and describes a process for identifying them within an information system. This section concludes with an explanation as to how these topics are related to the activities conducted during the workshop

3.2 NIST FIPS 199

NIST FIPS 199 defines an information type as a specific category of information (e.g., privacy, medical, proprietary, financial, investigative, contractor sensitive, security management), defined by an organization, or in some instances, by a specific law, Executive Order, directive, policy, or regulation [4]. This definition is particularly apt for public safety. The data handled by public safety will be subject to varying policy and regulations. It may change between public safety organizations, and it will differ based on the mission types of different public safety organizations. The workshop organizers narrowed this definition to included only information types that are retrieved by, stored on, or transmitted from a public safety mobile application

NIST FIPS 199 further states that each information type has a relationship with three core cybersecurity objectives:

- **Confidentiality** – preventing unauthorized disclosure of information;
- **Integrity** – preventing unauthorized modification of information; and
- **Availability** – providing timely access to information.

For each of these objectives, an information type is assigned an impact level of *low*, *moderate*, or *high*, depending on what security implications would result from a failure to achieve said objective.

- **Low** – limited adverse effect on organizational operations, organizational assets, or individuals resulting in minor degradation to an organization's ability to carry out its mission, minor financial loss, and/or minor harm to individuals.

- **Moderate** – serious adverse effect on organizational operations, organizational assets, or individuals including resulting in significant degradation to an organization's ability to carry out its mission, significant financial loss, and/or significant but non-life-threatening harm to individuals.

- **High** – severe or catastrophic effect on organizational operations, organizational assets, or individuals resulting in severe degradation to or a complete loss of an organization's ability to carry out its mission, severe financial loss, and/or catastrophic harm to individuals involving loss of life or serious life threatening injuries.

NIST FIPS 199 provides a compact representation for an information type's security categorization [7]:

> Security Category (SC) information type = {(**confidentiality**, *impact*), (**integrity**, *impact*), (**availability**, *impact*)}

Finally, NIST FIPS 199 describes applying a security categorization to an information system. U.S. law defines an information system as "a discrete set of information resources organized for the collection, processing, maintenance, use, sharing, or disposition of information" [8]. By this definition, a public safety mobile device is an information system. Applying a security categorization to an information system entails identifying the impact level for each of the cybersecurity objectives—confidentiality, integrity, and availability—for the information system. To do this, an organization must first identify each of the information type categorizations associated with that system. The highest impact level for each security objective becomes the impact level for that objective for the information system. This process is summarized in Figure 3-1:

> SC information type 1 = {(**confidentiality**, impact), (**integrity**, impact), (**availability**, impact)}
>
> SC information type 2 = {(**confidentiality**, impact), (**integrity**, impact), (**availability**, impact)}
>
> ...
>
> SC information type n = {(**confidentiality**, impact), (**integrity**, impact), (**availability**, impact)}
>
> SC information system = {(**confidentiality**, highest impact),
>
> (**integrity**, highest impact),
>
> (**availability**, highest impact)}

Figure 3-1 Categorizing an Information System

3.3 NIST Risk Management Framework

The NIST Risk Management Framework (RMF) describes the processes through which an organization manages risk to the organization or to individuals associated with the operation of an information system [4]. The RMF describes the risk associated with an information system as being a measure of two components [3]:

- The adverse impacts that would arise should there be a compromise to confidentiality, integrity, or availability to an information system; and

- The likelihood of such an occurrence.

The RMF establishes a life cycle for managing the risk associated with an information system. Figure 3-2 is an overview of the steps involved in the cycle. The first phase in this cycle is the categorization of the information system in the manner described in Section 3.2. Based on how the system is categorized, an organization must then select and develop appropriate security controls to safeguard the system. Once these controls have been implemented, assessed, and approved the information system is authorized for operation. The final phase in the cycle is to monitor the information system. Monitoring helps determine if the deployed security controls continue to be effective over time. It also addresses the inevitable changes to hardware, firmware, and operational environment that the system can experience during the lifetime of the system's deployment. Rather than being a terminating state for the RMF, the monitor phase requires a continuous effort. Any changes to a system's categorization or security controls determined to be ineffective trigger a new iteration through the RMF life cycle.

Figure 3-2 NIST Risk Management Framework Security Life Cycle [6]

The first step in this cycle was the focus of the workshop. NIST SP 800-60 Volume I Revision 1, *Guide for Mapping Types of Information and Information System Categories* [6], provides guidance on the first step of the RMF Security Life Cycle by subdividing it into four steps:

1. Identify Information Types,
2. Select Provisional Impact Levels,
3. Review and Adjust Impact Levels, and
4. Assign System Security Impact Category.

Steps 1 and 2 were the specific activities carried out during the workshop.

The guideline identifies two general information type classes to consider when dissecting an information system. The first, mission based information describes information relating to the core functions defined by the given mission of an organization. This includes both the services provided by an organization as well as the methods through which those services are delivered. The second, management and support based information, entails information relating to organizational functions that support the primary missions of an organization. Table 3-1 contains several federal information types identified in NIST SP 800-60.

Table 3-1 Selected Federal Information Types

Mission based	Border and Transportation Security	Judicial Hearings
	Criminal Apprehension	Postal Services
	Disaster Preparedness and Planning	Strategic National and Theater Defense
	Energy Production	
	Intelligence Planning	
Management and Support Based	Budget Formulation	IT Infrastructure Management
	Strategic Planning	Goods acquisition
	HR Strategy	

Finally, NIST SP 800-60 identifies two important concepts when considering the impact level of an information systems and information types. One concept is the security implications of an information type might change as a function of time (typically becoming less sensitive the older they become). The other is that information types that are categorized one way when examined independently may have greater security implications when provided in the context of other information types.

3.4 Defining Data Type

Both NIST SP 800-60 and FIPS 199 treat information types as the atomic units when describing cybersecurity risk. They describe information types from an organizationally top-down perspective and use them to encapsulate broad categories of information. Conversely, for the workshop, attendees were asked to treat an information type using a bottom-up approach. Rather than starting with the organization and drilling down to look for information types, they were asked to start with public safety tasks (scenarios) and aggregate up. The term data type was presented to workshop attendees as a stand-in for information type. Data types are synonymous with smaller, more specific instances of information. By focusing on data types, rather than information types, the workshop organizers hoped to focus more closely on specific mobile application usage and functionality. These data types still fit into the operations described in NIST SP 800-60 and FIPS 199 because they are, by their nature, subcomponents of the broader information type concept. The actual definition for a data type provided for use during the workshop is as follows:

1. *A specific category of information defined by an organization, or in some instances by law, Executive Order, directive, policy, or regulation*

2. *Any type of information that can be delivered to, stored on, or transmitted from a public safety mobile device.*

3.5 Tying Everything Together

To reiterate, the goal of the workshop was to identify data types used by public safety mobile applications. Figure 3-3 provides an overview of how the parts described in this section fit together. By treating public safety mobile devices and applications as information systems the NIST Risk Management Framework can be used to strengthen an organization's cybersecurity posture. The entry point into the RMF entails categorizing the information system. The workshop focused on two steps described by NIST SP 800-60 that make up this first stage. The first was identifying data types by leveraging the description of an information type described in FIPS 199 and enhancing it to better fit the workshop's need. The second was using the method described in FIPS 199 to apply security categorizations to the identified data types.

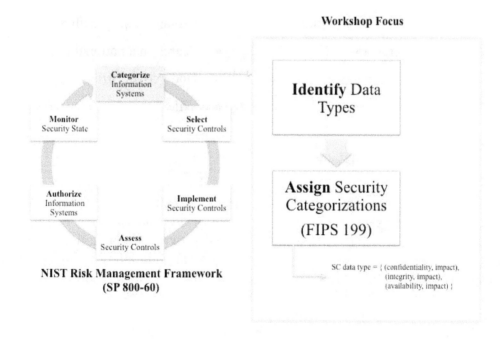

Figure 3-3 Workshop Methodology Overview

4. Workshop Structure

The exercise that drove our workshop was designed to allow attendees to utilize their domain knowledge of different public safety roles and functions to enumerate data types that will be associated with public safety mobile devices. The workshop had two major goals:

- Identifying data types that will be handled on public safety mobile devices, and
- Categorizing those data types based on the cybersecurity risk.

The workshop was divided into two main phases. Phase one involved dividing the workshop into two groups. Each group was tasked with evaluating the same public safety scenario: *explosion at a chemical plant*. Each group independently attempted to identify and categorize as many data types appropriate to the scenario as they could. The groups then compared and contrasted each of the data types examined. Phase two involved breaking the workshop into groups of 4 to 6 individuals. Each group was assigned different scenarios. As in the first phase, each group attempted to identify as many data types as possible. To end the workshop, each group shared their findings.

The following scenarios were used to frame these discussions, detailed explanations of which can be found in Appendix A—.

- Explosion at a chemical plant
- Medical Emergency
- Rioting in an urban area
- Structure fire
- Hurricane
- Police officer vehicle stop

- Personal injury with hazards
- Search in a national park
- Undercover officer
- Wild fire
- Active shooter

To avoid getting distracted by out of scope details such as device manufacturer, device form factor, mobile application operating system, etc., participants were asked to imagine they had "the perfect app(s) on the perfect device." Attendees were then presented with various predefined public safety scenarios. For each scenario attendees were asked what types of public safety roles, functions, and information they envisioned their devices would handle. Attendees were encouraged to imagine new or desirable functionality they wished to see in future mobile apps. Workshop facilitators then used the attendees' input to extract associated public safety data types. Finally, attendees were asked to use their domain knowledge of public safety's mission to apply security categorizations to each of the identified information types.

5.   Identified Data Types and Categorizations

5.1   Overall Totals

This section describes the data types captured by the workshop. Overall workshop attendees were able to identify 109 unique data types. Of those types 76 data types were assigned security categorizations. The remaining 33 types were left uncategorized due to time constraints on the workshop. These figures are captured in Table 5-1

Table 5-1 Data Type Counts

Identified Data Types	109
Categorized Data Types	76
Uncategorized Data Types	33

As explained in Section 3.2, each data type is given an impact level for each of the three security objectives. Examining the number of instances each of the impact levels shows the impact trend for data types for public safety. Because there were 76 categorized data types and each type is given an impact type for the three security objectives, there were 228 impact levels observed. Of the categorized types, workshop attendees heavily favored the high impact classification, using it 154 times. The moderate and low impact classifications were applied roughly the same number of times, being used 34 and 50 times respectively. These results are summarized in Figure 5-1.

Examining the impact count when grouped by security objectives shows how the attendees viewed the importance of each of objective. Figure 5-2 summarizes this grouping. As shown, the attendees favored the high impact classification over moderate and low for all three security objectives. The grouping also reveals that many more of the categorized data types have high impact classifications for integrity and availability.

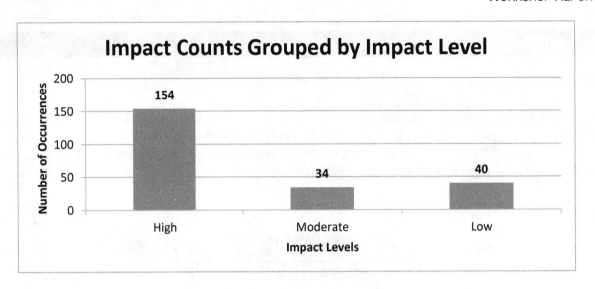

Figure 5-1 Impact Level Overall Totals

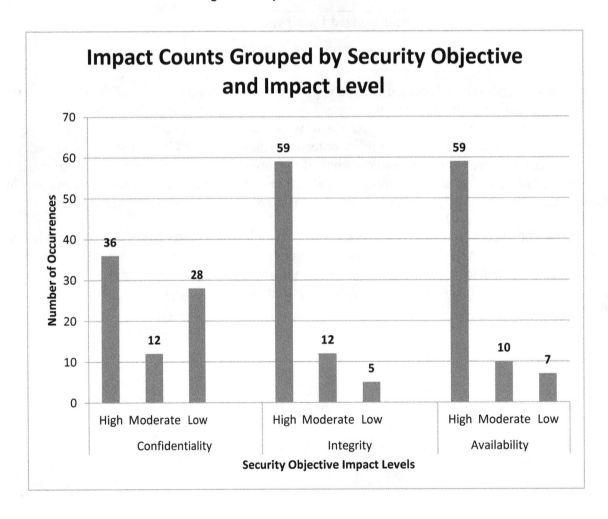

Figure 5-2 Impact Counts Organized by Security Objective and Impact Level

As a post-workshop exercise, the workshop organizers grouped the information types identified during the workshop into four broad categories:

- Operations Data,
- Situational Awareness Data,
- Sensor Data, and
- Publicly Sourced Data.

The remainder of this section will define each of these categories and examine the impact breakdown of the information types included in each.

5.2 Operations Data

Workshop organizers defined operations data as information used directly by public safety command and control for active operations. These information types included incident action plans, the location and distribution of deployable assets, white boarding information, etc. Information types in the operations data category tended toward impact classifications of high for confidentiality, integrity, and availability. An overview of the totals for each of operations data types as grouped by security objective, and then impact level can be found in Figure 5-3. The full list of identified operations data types can be found in Table 5-2.

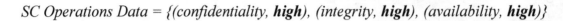

*SC Operations Data = {(confidentiality, **high**), (integrity, **high**), (availability, **high**)}*

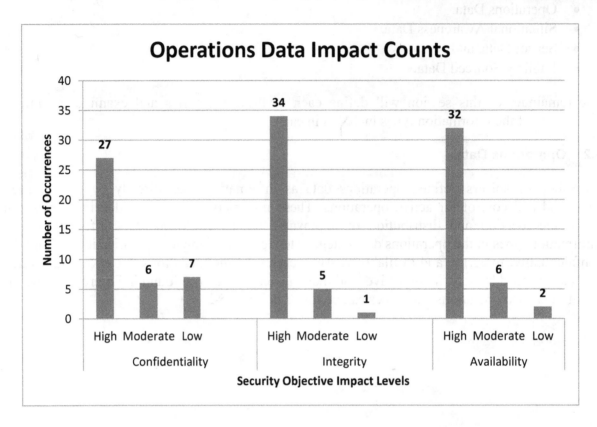

Number of Operations Data Types	40	Impact Level Totals	
		High	93
		Moderate	17
		Low	10

Figure 5-3 Operations Data Totals

Table 5-2 Operations Data Types and Categorizations

h – high impact   m – moderate impact   l – low impact

Information Type	Impact		
	Confidentiality	Integrity	Availability
active authentication	h	h	h
body camera data	h	h	h
comms	h	h	h
completed incident command system (ICS) forms/plans	h	h	h
crime scene geographic information system (GIS) intel location	h	h	h
critical static locations (shelters|ccps|EVAC|LZ)	h	m	m
deployable assets	h	h	h
Emergency Response	l	h	h
evac routes and plans	l	h	h
facial recognition	h	h	m
first responder assets	h	h	h
functional roles	m	h	h
ICS (incident command system) forms/plans	h	h	h
images + media from ng911	l	m	h
incident action plan	h	h	h
Info from multiple CAD LE Location	h	m	h
law enforcement intel	h	h	h
license and plate reader	m	h	l
license plate recognition (LPR)	h	h	h
managing security	h	h	h

patient information	h	h	m
patient quarantine (no PII)	l	h	h
patient triage	m	h	h
personnel on-site	m	h	m
photo's video audio (of target suspects)	h	h	h
point of contacts	m	h	h
pre-plans (PII)	h	h	h
resident contact info	m	h	h
responder camera	h	h	h
responding assets	h	h	h
response markers/location	h	m	m
search status for secondary explosive devices	h	h	h
security check point locations	h	h	h
social media push	l	h	h
tactical command and control	h	h	h
victims/casualties	h	h	h
white boarding	h	h	h
video data analysis	h	h	h
video	l	l	l
video/photos	l	m	m

5.3 Situational Awareness Data

Situational awareness data was defined as information types used to augment a first responder's understanding of contextual situations. These information types included both static resources like topological maps, satellite imagery, and building blueprints, but also dynamic types such as real time hospital capacity, flight traffic from the Federal Aviation Administration (FAA), traffic information from local transportation departments. These information types were separated from the operations data category because they typically represent information sources that already exist digitally from external sources. It was observed also that information types of this category tended to have lower impact on confidentially while maintaining the high integrity and availability impact levels from the previous category. Figure 5-4 describes the total counts for the data types in this category grouped by security objective and then impact level. A full list of all the data types in this category can be found in Table 5-3.

*SC Situational Awareness Data = {(confidentiality, **low**), (integrity, **high**),*

*(availability, **high**)}*

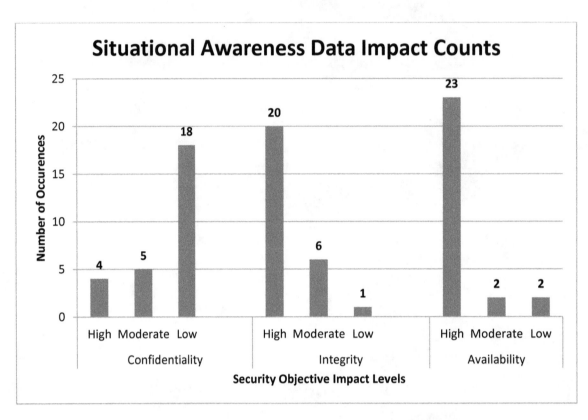

Number of Situational Awareness Data Types	27	Impact Level Totals	
		High	47
		Moderate	13
		Low	21

Figure 5-4 Situational Awareness Totals

Table 5-3 Situational Awareness Data Types and Categorizations

h – high impact   m – moderate impact   l – low impact

	Impact		
Information Type	**Confidentiality**	**Integrity**	**Availability**
Blueprints	m	h	h
building footprints	l	h	h
critical infrastructure(CI) around location geomapping	h	h	h
critical logistics stations	m	h	h
department of transportation (DoT) logistic info	l	h	h
elevation model	l	h	h
environmental conditions	l	m	h
event location	l	h	h
flight traffic/FAA information	l	l	l
fuel sources	l	h	h
ground cover	l	h	h
hazardous materials	m	h	h
hospital bed counts	l	m	m
hospital capacity	m	h	h
Hydrants	l	m	h
impact map/plume model	l	h	h
maps	l	h	h
medical facility bed count	l	h	h
satellite imagery	l	h	h
shelter	l	h	h
standing water	l	h	h
traffic-surface	l	m	l

utility information	h	h	h
utility logistic info	m	h	h
video from security cameras	h	h	h
video around location	h	m	m
weather	l	m	h

5.4 Sensor Data

Sensor data describes telemetry generated via sensors worn by first responders in the field. Data such as responder status monitoring, equipment status sensors, etc., fall into this category. The full list of information types in this category can be found in Table 5-4. Information types in this category share many characteristics with operations data but were separated into a different category because they represent data associated with individual first responders. Like operations data, sensor data tended to carry the high impact classifier for all three security objectives. Figure 5-5 describes the total counts for the data types in this category grouped by security objective and then impact level.

*SC Sensor Data = {(confidentiality, **high**), (integrity, **high**), (availability, **high**)}*

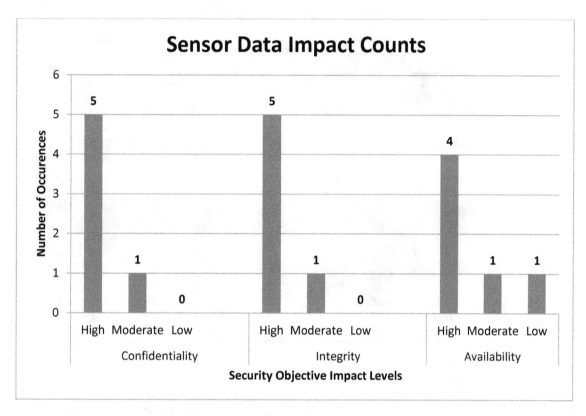

Number of Sensor Data Types	6	Impact Level Totals	
		High	14
		Moderate	3
		Low	1

Figure 5-5 Sensor Data Totals

Table 5-4 Sensor Data Types and Categorizations

	h – high impact m – moderate impact l – low impact		
		Impact	
Information Type	**Confidentiality**	**Integrity**	**Availability**
environmental sensor data	m	h	h
equipment/smartsensor	h	h	m
geo data / accelerometer	h	m	l
location GPS	h	h	h
officer status - sensor monitoring	h	h	h
personal protective equipment (PPE) responder biometric sensors	h	h	h

5.5   Publicly Sourced Data

Publicly sourced data represented the smallest category identified by the workshop organizers. Information types in this category represent data coming either directly from social media or outside organizations that process social media for public safety. The full list of information types in this category can be found in Table 5-5. There was a consensus among attendees data of this type would have value but mostly as supplemental information to their operations. This manifested in low impact classifications for confidentiality, integrity, and availability. Figure 5-6 describes the total counts for the data types in this category grouped by security objective and then impact level.

*SC Publicly Sourced Data = {(confidentiality, **low**), (integrity, **low**), (availability, **low**)}*

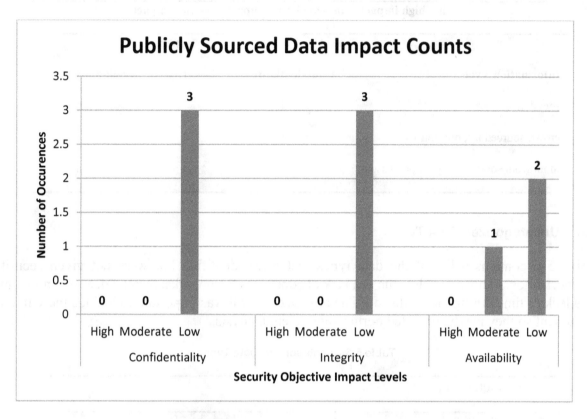

Number of Public Safety Data Types	3	Impact Level Totals	
		High	0
		Moderate	1
		Low	8

Figure 5-6 Publicly Sourced Data Totals

Table 5-5 Publicly Sourced Data Types and Categorizations

	h – high impact	m – moderate impact	l – low impact

| Information Type | Impact | | |
	Confidentiality	Integrity	Availability
social media	l	l	m
crowd sourced information	l	l	l
input from social media pre processors	l	l	l

5.6 Uncategorized Data Types

Table 5-6 contains a list of the data types that were identified but were not given security categorizations. This was either due to a lack of consensus from workshop attendees or simply due to a lack of time during the workshop. The organizers felt it was important to include these in this document so they maybe revisited during subsequent analysis.

Table 5-6 Uncategorized Data Types

accelerometer data
active authentication
blueprints of the facility
chem track
common operational picture
critical locations
Damage assessments
domosf needs assessment
ERG - (Emergency Response Guide) and PPE (Personal Protective Equipment)
evacuation routes
event location
environmental conditions

FF sensors (biometrics and equipment)

impact model (plume model)

incident management

Information about suspects

law enforcement intel

location of caller

location of responders

medical facility bed count

NG9-1-1

patient info casualties

personnel on site (employees and visitors)

physical asset inventory

physical asset location

plant inventory

street traffic

types of hazardous materials

utilities

utility info - hot wires

white force locator

Appendix A—Workshop Scenarios

A.1   Scenario: Explosion at a chemical plant

A large explosion occurs at a chemical plant in a suburb. A potential exists for hazardous chemical leaks as well as toxic smoke emissions from the burning chemicals. Multiple employees are severely injured from the initial blast, and part of the plant is on fire. Plant security officers call 9-1-1, triggering a response from police, fire, EMS, and emergency management personnel.

Considerations:

- A shopping area is near the chemical plant.

- The chemical plant has a security cameras and a fenced perimeter with access by a four-digit code.

- Off-duty personnel with Hazardous Materials (HazMat) and Urban Search and Rescue (USaR) training are called in from surrounding jurisdictions.

- The plant has created digital maps of each floor, including sub-ground levels and parking garages.

- Wireless sensors on fire fighter gear detect hazardous chemicals.

- Law enforcement coordinates with the Dept. of Transportation to divert traffic away from the incident.

- Emergency medicine coordinates with utilities to manage power lines knocked down by the explosion and affected gas lines.

- Incident command suspects the explosion was not an accident and detectives are assigned to begin an investigation in coordination with fire investigators.

- After determining that the probable cause of the explosion was a bomb, incident command initiates a secondary device search by the Explosive Ordinance Disposal team.

- Nearby medical facilities cannot handle the casualties.

- Some responders are using personal devices

- Some responders are using the FirstNet network and others are using commercial networks

A.2   Scenario: Personal Injury Collision with hazards

A high-speed collision between a propane tanker and a sport utility vehicle (SUV) has occurred on a major highway during rush hour. The tanker is now lying on its side blocking three of the four southbound lanes and is leaking propane on the highway. Four other vehicles suffered subsequent accidents as a result of the primary incident.

Sample Information Types:

- Tanker contents.

- Vehicle telematics (speed, number of occupants, make/model, etc.).

- Miscellaneous assets (tow trucks, flat-bed trucks, MCI bus, etc.).

Considerations:

- Members of the public could benefit from knowing how to manage the hazardous materials before first responders are able to advise them.

- Reviewing vehicle schematics while en route could help responders prepare for an extrication. The make/model might come from Machine to Machine (M2M) or citizen report.

A.3   Scenario: Medical emergency

During a medical emergency response, a paramedic uses an app to collect a patient's information (name, age, gender, age, etc.), record the patient's vital signs (heart rate, blood pressure, temperature, etc.), and look up medications. In addition, the app forwards the patient information to the hospital the patient will be taken to.

Sample Information Types:

- Patient information and vitals.

- Hospital statuses.

- Publicly accessible automated external defibrillator locations.

Considerations:

- Do the responder and hospital need the same app to share the information?

- How sensitive is information about communicable diseases? Does it matter whether the patient is in public or at home?

A.4   Scenario: Search in a national park

After firing on police, an armed and violent fugitive has taken refuge in a national park. The park, located about 48 km (approx. 30 miles) north of Harrisburg, is about 72.8 km^2 (approx. 28 square miles) in area. It is heavily wooded and crisscrossed with biking/hiking trails.

Sample Information Types:

- Search team assignment.

- Officer location.

- Maps describing the search progress.

- Pictures of the fugitive.

- Body cam video.

Considerations:

- What changes if the search is for a missing person rather than a fugitive?

A.5   Scenario: Rioting in an urban area

Police are struggling to contain a riot downtown that has sparked looting and multiple structure and vehicle fires. EMTs will be deployed to aid injured citizens and potentially injured public safety actors.

Sample Information Types:

- Activity hot zones.

- Officer distress alerts.

- City maps.

Considerations:

- Does the assessment change when an injured Law Enforcement Officer (LEO) is the patient?

- Does the assessment change when helpful information about ongoing and anticipated incidents can be crowd sourced?

A.6   Scenario: Undercover officer

As part of a covert operation, an undercover officer is using a mobile application on his/her mobile device to provide operation information back to the operation's command center.

Sample Information Types:

- Confidential informant information.

- Video, voice, location, etc., from the officer.

Considerations:

- What if the undercover officer is compromised?

A.7 Scenario: Structure fire

During a response to a building fire, a firefighter uses an app on his/her mobile device to navigate through the building as well as provide firefighter location to the fire incident commander.

Sample Information Types:

- Hydrant locations.

- Utility shutoffs.

- Unique hazards (propane tanks, lack of standpipes, etc.).

- Building occupancy.

Considerations:

- Does the assessment change if the structure is a small house vs. apartment vs. commercial structure?

A.8 Scenario: Wild fire

A wildfire is steadily approaching a residential neighborhood of about two hundred family homes. Firefighters are working to contain the fire, but the decision is made to evacuate the adjacent neighborhood.

Sample Information Types:

- Weather conditions/forecast (prevailing winds, rain, etc.).

- Residential maps.

- Residential alert check-off list.

- Topological information.

Considerations:

- Residents might more readily evacuate with more information from fire operations.

A.9   Scenario: Hurricane

A hurricane struck several states, causing significant damage and knocking out power for several days.

Sample Information Types:

- Deployable assets (generators, Cell on Wheels, etc.).

- Disaster relief volunteers.

- Shelter location and status.

- Residents who need oxygen or batteries for their wheel chairs.

Considerations:

- First responders (both on and off duty) coordinate safety checks with community organizations.

A.10   Scenario: Active shooter

During an active shooter incident, a person on scene uses an app to send video of the shooter.

Sample Information Types:

- Suspect description and location.

- Victim and survivor information (emergency contacts, medical history, etc.).

Considerations:

- Does the assessment change if in a school vs. in a mall?

A.11   Scenario: Police officer vehicle stop

On a traffic stop, an officer uses an app to contact the communications center and check out the vehicle, provide the location, a vehicle description, and run the license plate and driver ID against local, State, and Federal records.

Sample Information Types:

- Officer ID and location.

- Dash cam feed.

- Nearby traffic cameras.

- Vehicle and suspect information (including biometric identifiers).

- Stolen vehicle and criminal records databases.

- IoT (Internet of Things—officer vitals monitor, holster sensor, etc.).

- Nearby units to assist if required/requested.

Considerations:

- Does the assessment change if:

  o Shots are fired;

  o The suspect flees after initially stopping; or

  o The driver or vehicle returns a "hit" for a warrant, stolen vehicle, or other officer safety issue.

Appendix B—References

[1]   Federal Information Security Management Act of 2002, Pub. L. 107-347
         (Title III), 116 Stat. 2946. http://www.gpo.gov/fdsys/pkg/PLAW-
         107publ347/pdf/PLAW-107publ347.pdf.

[2]   FirstNet, *Appendix C-10 NPSBN Cyber Security*, October 5, 2015.
         https://www.fbo.gov/utils/view?id=9742a7b4b8e353a09effc4f826
         65d453 (accessed 5/25/2016).

[3]   Joint Task Force Transformation Initiative, *Guide for Conducting Risk
         Assessments*, NIST Special Publication (SP) 800-30 Revision 1, September
         2012. http://dx.doi.org/10.6028/NIST.SP.800-30r1.

[4]   National Institute of Standards and Technology, *Risk Management
         Framework (RMF) Overview* [Web page], April 1, 2014.
         http://csrc.nist.gov/groups/SMA/fisma/framework.html (accessed
         5/25/2016).

[5]   M. Ogata, B. Guttman, and N. Hastings, *Public Safety Mobile Application
         Security Requirements Workshop Summary*, NISTIR 8018, January 2015.
         http://dx.doi.org/10.6028/NIST.IR.8018.

[6]   K. Stine, R. Kissel, W. C. Barker, J. Fahlsing, and J. Gulick, *Guide for
         Mapping Types of Information and Information Systems to Security
         Categories*, NIST Special Publication (SP) 800-60 Volume I, Revision 1,
         August 2008. http://dx.doi.org/10.6028/NIST.SP.800-60v1r1.

[7]   National Institute of Standards and Technology, *Standards for Security
         Categorization of Federal Information and Information Systems*, Federal
         Information Processing Standard (FIPS) 199, February 2004.
         http://csrc.nist.gov/publications/fips/fips199/FIPS-PUB-199-final.pdf
         (accessed 5/25/2016).

[8]   44 U.S.C., §3502 (2014). https://www.gpo.gov/fdsys/pkg/USCODE-2014-
         title44/pdf/USCODE-2014-title44-chap35.pdf (accessed 5/25/2016).